The Little Old Fashioned Recipe Book

MYTHIC MIXOLOGY
Cocktail Recipes for Nerds

Cocktail recipes curated for enthusiasts and nerds alike. Drawing inspiration from themes of science fiction, enchanting realms of fantasy, rich tapestries of literature, and the intricate annals of world histories.

The Little Old Fashioned

Fashioned

Recipe Book

Over 50 Unique Old
Fashioned Recipes

Table of Contents

Introduction

Hey there, cocktail lovers! Welcome to "The Little Old Fashioned Recipe Book," where we take you on a trip down memory lane, clinking glasses with one of the oldest and most cherished cocktails around: the Old Fashioned. This book is all about celebrating the drink's rich history, unlocking its timeless flavors, and offering a variety of twists that bring this classic into the modern day.

First, let's raise a glass to the Old Fashioned's humble beginnings. Back in the late 1800s, mixology was just getting its footing, and the Old Fashioned was a breath of fresh air. It was a response to all the complex, overly frilly cocktails popping up, bringing the focus back to simple, balanced ingredients: whiskey, bitters, sugar, and water. That classic combo laid the groundwork for countless variations to come, proving that sometimes less is more.

In a world where cocktails can get pretty wild with their ingredients, the Old Fashioned is a soothing reminder of the joys of simplicity. It's about balance, ritual, and connection – between the bartender and drinker, and between the drinker and the drink. Making an Old Fashioned isn't just about mixing a cocktail; it's about creating an experience. It's about savoring each sip and enjoying the journey it takes you on.

So, what's in store for you in this book? We've got a whole bunch of recipes to explore. We'll start with the classic Old Fashioned, helping you master its timeless elegance. Then, we'll dive into regional twists, showcasing how different areas put their own unique spin on the drink, from a Southern sweet tea-infused version to a brandy-based Midwest favorite.

We've got recipes for every season too, from autumnal spice-infused variations to refreshing summer twists. And, for those who love a bit of innovation, we've got contemporary takes that blend classic techniques with modern ingredients, like smoked bitters and craft syrups. Finally, we explore global inspirations, like a Japanese whiskey and yuzu bitters blend or a Caribbean rum twist, showing just how adaptable this cocktail really is.

Now, crafting an Old Fashioned is an art. We'll guide you through each step, from picking the right whiskey to choosing the perfect bitters, sugar, and garnishes. And don't worry, we've got you covered on techniques like muddling and stirring, ensuring you get the perfect balance every time. Presentation is key too, and we'll show you how to serve and garnish your cocktail in style.

The Old Fashioned has stood the test of time, transcending trends to become a staple in bars and homes alike. Its ability to adapt and evolve, while staying true to its roots, makes it a timeless favorite. So, whether you're a seasoned mixologist or a newbie looking to experiment, this book has something for you. Raise a glass, savor the flavors, and let's embark on a journey through the world of the Old Fashioned, celebrating its elegance and versatility along the way. Cheers!

A Little Old Fashioned

Ladies and gentlemen, take a seat at the cocktail bar, because we're about to delve into the sophisticated world of the Old Fashioned. It's one of the classics, a true gem of the cocktail world, and the drink of choice for many a discerning drinker. But what makes this timeless concoction so special? Let's break down the recipe, exploring what each ingredient brings to the table.

An Old Fashioned, at its core, consists of a few simple ingredients: 2 oz of whiskey, 1 sugar cube or 1/2 oz of simple syrup, 2-3 dashes of bitters, and an orange peel for garnish. The whiskey is the bold, smooth base that forms the foundation of the Old Fashioned. Traditionally, bourbon or rye whiskey is used, each bringing its own character. Bourbon offers a sweeter, mellow base, with notes of vanilla, caramel, and oak, while rye whiskey introduces a spicier, drier flavor, with hints of pepper, spices, and a drier finish, perfect for those who prefer a punchier Drink.

The sugar, whether in the form of a cube or simple syrup, serves as the sweetener, balancing out the warmth of the whiskey. The sweetness softens the drink's edges, making it smoother and more palatable. A few dashes of bitters then transform the Old Fashioned from a simple whiskey cocktail into a complex, nuanced drink, adding depth and balancing the sweetness. Aromatic bitters bring hints of spices, herbs, and botanicals, enhancing the drink's overall flavor profile, while other bitters, such as orange or chocolate, can offer unique twists.

Finally, the orange peel garnish provides a fragrant citrus aroma that hits the nose before the first sip. The essential oils released from twisting the peel over the drink give it a bright, zesty finish, bringing everything together in a harmonious way. This classic cocktail proves that sometimes simplicity breeds sophistication, creating a timeless drink that has delighted palates for generations. So next time you raise an Old Fashioned, take a moment to appreciate its ingredients and the harmony they bring to your glass.

Recipes

Absinthe Old Fashioned

- ➤ *1 sugar cube*
- ➤ *4-6 dashes of Angostura bitters*
- ➤ *2 oz rye whiskey or bourbon*
- ➤ *1 bar spoon of absinthe*
- ➤ *Ice cubes*
- ➤ *Orange twist*

Preparation: Place the sugar cube in an Old Fashioned glass.

Bitters: Douse the sugar cube with bitters, making sure it's fully saturated.

Muddle: Muddle the sugar cube until it dissolves, creating a sweet and spicy mixture.

Whiskey: Add the whiskey or bourbon, stirring well until fully integrated.

Absinthe: Pour the absinthe over the back of a spoon into the mixture, letting it mix thoroughly.

Ice: Add a few ice cubes to chill and dilute the drink slightly.

Garnish: Express the oils of an orange twist over the drink, and then drop it into the glass.

Serve: Stir well, and enjoy!

Agave Old Fashioned

- ➤ I sugar cube
- ➤ 1/4 oz agave syrup
- ➤ 4-6 dashes of Angostura bitters
- ➤ 2 oz tequila
- ➤ Ice cubes
- ➤ Orange or lemon twist

Sugar: If using a sugar cube, place it in an Old Fashioned glass and douse with bitters, then muddle until fully dissolved. If using agave syrup, add it directly to the glass along with the bitters, and stir to combine.

Tequila: Add the tequila to the glass, stirring until fully integrated.

Ice: Add a few ice cubes, stirring gently to chill and dilute the drink slightly.

Garnish: Express the oils of an orange or lemon twist over the drink, and then drop it into the glass.

Serve: Stir well, and enjoy!

Almond Old Fashioned

- ➤ I sugar cube
- ➤ 1/4 oz almond syrup
- ➤ 4-6 dashes of Angostura bitters
- ➤ 2 oz bourbon or rye whiskey
- ➤ Ice cubes
- ➤ Orange twist

Sugar: If using a sugar cube, place it in an Old Fashioned glass and douse with bitters, then muddle until fully dissolved. If using almond syrup, add it directly to the glass along with the bitters, and stir to combine.

Whiskey: Add the bourbon or rye whiskey to the glass, stirring until fully integrated.

Ice: Add a few ice cubes, stirring gently to chill and dilute the drink slightly.

Garnish: Express the oils of an orange twist over the drink, and then drop it into the glass.

Serve: Stir well, and enjoy!

Apple Cider Old Fashioned

- 1/4 oz simple syrup or 1 sugar cube
- 4-6 dashes of Angostura bitters
- 1 oz apple cider
- 2 oz bourbon or rye whiskey
- Ice cubes
- Orange twist or apple slice

Sugar: If using a sugar cube, place it in an Old Fashioned glass and douse with bitters, then muddle until fully dissolved. If using simple syrup, add it directly to the glass along with the bitters, and stir to combine.

Apple Cider: Add the apple cider to the glass, stirring until integrated.

Whiskey: Add the bourbon or rye whiskey, stirring until fully integrated.

Ice: Add a few ice cubes, stirring gently to chill and dilute the drink slightly.

Garnish: Express the oils of an orange twist over the drink, and then drop it into the glass, or add an apple slice.

Serve: Stir well, and enjoy!

Balsamic Old Fashioned

- ➤ *1 sugar cube or 1/4 oz simple syrup*
- ➤ *4-6 dashes of Angostura bitters*
- ➤ *1/4 oz aged balsamic vinegar*
- ➤ *2 oz bourbon or rye whiskey*
- ➤ *Ice cubes*
- ➤ *Orange twist*

Sugar: If using a sugar cube, place it in an Old Fashioned glass and douse with bitters, then muddle until fully dissolved. If using simple syrup, add it directly to the glass along with the bitters, and stir to combine.

Balsamic: Add the balsamic vinegar to the glass, stirring until well mixed.

Whiskey: Add the bourbon or rye whiskey to the glass, stirring until fully integrated.

Ice: Add a few ice cubes, stirring gently to chill and dilute the drink slightly.

Garnish: Express the oils of an orange twist over the drink, and then drop it into the glass.

Serve: Stir well, and enjoy!

Banana Old Fashioned

- I sugar cube or 1/4 oz simple syrup
- 4-6 dashes of Angostura bitters
- 1/4 oz banana liqueur
- 2 oz bourbon or rye whiskey
- Ice cubes
- Orange twist or banana slice

Sugar: If using a sugar cube, place it in an Old Fashioned glass and douse with bitters, then muddle until fully dissolved. If using simple syrup, add it directly to the glass along with the bitters, and stir to combine.

Banana Liqueur: Add the banana liqueur to the glass, stirring until well mixed.

Whiskey: Add the bourbon or rye whiskey to the glass, stirring until fully integrated.

Ice: Add a few ice cubes, stirring gently to chill and dilute the drink slightly.

Garnish: Express the oils of an orange twist over the drink, and then drop it into the glass, or add a slice of banana.

Serve: Stir well, and enjoy!

Basil Old Fashioned

- ➤ 1 sugar cube or 1/4 oz simple syrup
- ➤ 4-6 dashes of Angostura bitters
- ➤ 2 oz bourbon or rye whiskey
- ➤ 1-2 basil leaves
- ➤ Ice cubes
- ➤ Orange twist or basil leaf

Sugar: If using a sugar cube, place it in an Old Fashioned glass and douse with bitters, then muddle until fully dissolved. If using simple syrup, add it directly to the glass along with the bitters, and stir to combine.

Basil: Add the basil leaves to the glass and muddle gently to release their flavor.

Whiskey: Add the bourbon or rye whiskey to the glass, stirring until fully integrated.

Ice: Add a few ice cubes, stirring gently to chill and dilute the drink slightly.

Garnish: Express the oils of an orange twist over the drink, and then drop it into the glass, or garnish with a fresh basil leaf.

Serve: Stir well, and enjoy!

Beetroot Old Fashioned

- I sugar cube or 1/4 oz simple syrup
- 4-6 dashes of Angostura bitters
- 1 oz beet juice
- 2 oz bourbon or rye whiskey
- Ice cubes
- Orange twist or beet slice

Sugar: If using a sugar cube, place it in an Old Fashioned glass and douse with bitters, then muddle until fully dissolved. If using simple syrup, add it directly to the glass along with the bitters, and stir to combine.

Beet Juice: Add the beet juice to the glass, stirring until integrated.

Whiskey: Add the bourbon or rye whiskey to the glass, stirring until fully integrated.

Ice: Add a few ice cubes, stirring gently to chill and dilute the drink slightly.

Garnish: Express the oils of an orange twist over the drink, and then drop it into the glass, or add a slice of beetroot.

Serve: Stir well, and enjoy!

Berry Old Fashioned

- ➤ *1 sugar cube or 1/4 oz simple syrup*
- ➤ *4-6 dashes of Angostura bitters*
- ➤ *4-6 mixed berries*
- ➤ *2 oz bourbon or rye whiskey*
- ➤ *Ice cubes*
- ➤ *Orange twist or a few fresh berries*

Sugar: If using a sugar cube, place it in an Old Fashioned glass and douse with bitters, then muddle until fully dissolved. If using simple syrup, add it directly to the glass along with the bitters.

Berries: Add the mixed berries to the glass and muddle them to release their juice and flavor, combining them with the sugar or syrup.

Whiskey: Add the bourbon or rye whiskey to the glass, stirring until fully integrated.

Ice: Add a few ice cubes, stirring gently to chill and dilute the drink slightly.

Garnish: Express the oils of an orange twist over the drink, and then drop it into the glass, or garnish with a few fresh berries.

Serve: Stir well, and enjoy!

Black Pepper Old Fashioned

- ➤ 1 sugar cube or 1/4 oz simple syrup
- ➤ 4-6 dashes of Angostura bitters
- ➤ 1/2 tsp freshly ground black pepper
- ➤ 2 oz bourbon or rye whiskey
- ➤ Ice cubes
- ➤ Orange twist

Sugar: If using a sugar cube, place it in an Old Fashioned glass and douse with bitters, then muddle until fully dissolved. If using simple syrup, add it directly to the glass along with the bitters.

Pepper: Add the freshly ground black pepper to the glass, stirring until well mixed.

Whiskey: Add the bourbon or rye whiskey to the glass, stirring until fully integrated.

Ice: Add a few ice cubes, stirring gently to chill and dilute the drink slightly.

Garnish: Express the oils of an orange twist over the drink, and then drop it into the glass.

Serve: Stir well, and enjoy!

Blood Orange Old Fashioned

- ➤ *1 sugar cube or 1/4 oz simple syrup*
- ➤ *4-6 dashes of Angostura bitters*
- ➤ *1 oz blood orange juice*
- ➤ *2 oz bourbon or rye whiskey*
- ➤ *Ice cubes*
- ➤ *Blood orange slice or twist*

Sugar: If using a sugar cube, place it in an Old Fashioned glass and douse with bitters, then muddle until fully dissolved. If using simple syrup, add it directly to the glass along with the bitters, and stir to combine.

Blood Orange Juice: Add the blood orange juice to the glass, stirring until fully integrated.

Whiskey: Add the bourbon or rye whiskey to the glass, stirring until fully integrated.

Ice: Add a few ice cubes, stirring gently to chill and dilute the drink slightly.

Garnish: Express the oils of a blood orange twist over the drink, and then drop it into the glass, or garnish with a blood orange slice.

Serve: Stir well, and enjoy!

Blueberry Old Fashioned

- I sugar cube or 1/4 oz simple syrup
- 4-6 dashes of Angostura bitters
- 6-8 fresh blueberries
- 2 oz bourbon or rye whiskey
- Ice cubes
- Orange twist

Sugar: If using a sugar cube, place it in an Old Fashioned glass and douse with bitters, then muddle until fully dissolved. If using simple syrup, add it directly to the glass along with the bitters.

Blueberries: Add the fresh blueberries to the glass and muddle them to release their juice and flavor, combining them with the sugar or syrup.

Whiskey: Add the bourbon or rye whiskey to the glass, stirring until fully integrated.

Ice: Add a few ice cubes, stirring gently to chill and dilute the drink slightly.

Garnish: Express the oils of an orange twist over the drink, and then drop it into the glass, or garnish with a few fresh blueberries.

Serve: Stir well, and enjoy!

Bourbon Old Fashioned

- I sugar cube or 1/4 oz simple syrup
- 4-6 dashes of Angostura bitters
- 2 oz bourbon whiskey
- Ice cubes
- Orange twist

Sugar: If using a sugar cube, place it in an Old Fashioned glass and douse with bitters, then muddle until fully dissolved. If using simple syrup, add it directly to the glass along with the bitters, and stir to combine.

Bourbon: Add the bourbon whiskey to the glass, stirring until fully integrated.

Ice: Add a few ice cubes, stirring gently to chill and dilute the drink slightly.

Garnish: Express the oils of an orange twist over the drink, and then drop it into the glass.

Serve: Stir well, and enjoy!

Brandy Old Fashioned

- *1 sugar cube or 1/4 oz simple syrup*
- *4-6 dashes of Angostura bitters*
- *2 oz brandy*
- *Ice cubes*
- *Cherry and orange slice*

Sugar: If using a sugar cube, place it in an Old Fashioned glass and douse with bitters, then muddle until fully dissolved. If using simple syrup, add it directly to the glass along with the bitters.

Brandy: Add the brandy to the glass, stirring until fully integrated.

Ice: Add a few ice cubes, stirring gently to chill and dilute the drink slightly.

Garnish: Add a cherry and/or orange slice to the drink for a classic finish.

Serve: Stir well, and enjoy!

Buttered Old Fashioned

- 1/4 oz simple syrup or 1 sugar cube
- 4-6 dashes of Angostura bitters
- 1 tsp unsalted butter, melted
- 2 oz bourbon or rye whiskey
- Ice cubes
- Orange twist

Sugar: If using a sugar cube, place it in an Old Fashioned glass and douse with bitters, then muddle until fully dissolved. If using simple syrup, add it directly to the glass along with the bitters.

Butter: Add the melted butter to the glass, stirring to mix it with the sugar and bitters.

Whiskey: Add the bourbon or rye whiskey to the glass, stirring until fully integrated.

Ice: Add a few ice cubes, stirring gently to chill and dilute the drink slightly.

Garnish: Express the oils of an orange twist over the drink, and then drop it into the glass.

Serve: Stir well, and enjoy!

Campari Old Fashioned

- ➢ 1 sugar cube or 1/4 oz simple syrup
- ➢ 4-6 dashes of Angostura bitters
- ➢ 1/4 oz Campari
- ➢ 2 oz bourbon or rye whiskey
- ➢ Ice cubes
- ➢ Orange twist

Sugar: If using a sugar cube, place it in an Old Fashioned glass and douse with bitters, then muddle until fully dissolved. If using simple syrup, add it directly to the glass along with the bitters.

Campari: Add the Campari to the glass, stirring until well mixed.

Whiskey: Add the bourbon or rye whiskey to the glass, stirring until fully integrated.

Ice: Add a few ice cubes, stirring gently to chill and dilute the drink slightly.

Garnish: Express the oils of an orange twist over the drink, and then drop it into the glass.

Serve: Stir well, and enjoy!

Caramel Old Fashioned

- *1 sugar cube or 1/4 oz caramel syrup*
- *4-6 dashes of Angostura bitters*
- *2 oz bourbon or rye whiskey*
- *Ice cubes*
- *Orange twist*
- *Caramel syrup*

Sugar: If using a sugar cube, place it in an Old Fashioned glass and douse with bitters, then muddle until fully dissolved. If using caramel syrup, add it directly to the glass along with the bitters.

Whiskey: Add the bourbon or rye whiskey to the glass, stirring until fully integrated.

Ice: Add a few ice cubes, stirring gently to chill and dilute the drink slightly.

Garnish: Express the oils of an orange twist over the drink, and then drop it into the glass, and drizzle with caramel syrup.

Serve: Stir well, and enjoy!

Cardamom Old Fashioned

- 1 sugar cube or 1/4 oz simple syrup
- 4-6 dashes of Angostura bitters
- 1/4 tsp ground cardamom or 1 crushed cardamom pod
- 2 oz bourbon or rye whiskey
- Ice cubes
- Orange twist
- Crushed cardamom pod

Sugar: If using a sugar cube, place it in an Old Fashioned glass and douse with bitters, then muddle until fully dissolved. If using simple syrup, add it directly to the glass along with the bitters.

Cardamom: Add the ground cardamom or crushed cardamom pod to the glass, stirring until well mixed.

Whiskey: Add the bourbon or rye whiskey to the glass, stirring until fully integrated.

Ice: Add a few ice cubes, stirring gently to chill and dilute the drink slightly.

Garnish: Express the oils of an orange twist over the drink, and then drop it into the glass, and add a crushed cardamom pod.

Serve: Stir well, and enjoy!

Carrot Cake Old Fashioned

- I sugar cube or 1/4 oz simple syrup
- 4-6 dashes of Angostura bitters
- 1 oz carrot juice
- 1/4 oz cinnamon syrup
- 2 oz bourbon or rye whiskey
- Ice cubes
- Orange twist
- Cinnamon

Sugar: If using a sugar cube, place it in an Old Fashioned glass and douse with bitters, then muddle until fully dissolved. If using simple syrup, add it directly to the glass along with the bitters.

Carrot Juice: Add the carrot juice to the glass, stirring until well mixed.

Cinnamon Syrup: Add the cinnamon syrup to the glass, stirring until integrated.

Whiskey: Add the bourbon or rye whiskey to the glass, stirring until fully integrated.

Ice: Add a few ice cubes, stirring gently to chill and dilute the drink slightly.

Garnish: Express the oils of an orange twist over the drink, and then drop it into the glass, sprinkle with cinnamon.

Serve: Stir well, and enjoy!

Chai Old Fashioned

- *I sugar cube or 1/4 oz simple syrup*
- *4-6 dashes of Angostura bitters*
- *1/4 tsp chai spice blend (or I chai tea bag)*
- *2 oz bourbon or rye whiskey*
- *Ice cubes*
- *Orange twist*

Sugar: If using a sugar cube, place it in an Old Fashioned glass and douse with bitters, then muddle until fully dissolved. If using simple syrup, add it directly to the glass along with the bitters.

Chai: Add the chai spice blend to the glass, or steep a chai tea bag in the bourbon or rye whiskey for 1-2 minutes, and then add the chai-infused whiskey to the glass.

Whiskey: If not already added, add the bourbon or rye whiskey to the glass, stirring until fully integrated.

Ice: Add a few ice cubes, stirring gently to chill and dilute the drink slightly.

Garnish: Express the oils of an orange twist over the drink, and then drop it into the glass.

Serve: Stir well, and enjoy!

Chamomile Old Fashioned

- *I sugar cube or 1/4 oz simple syrup*
- *4-6 dashes of Angostura bitters*
- *I oz chamomile tea or I chamomile tea bag*
- *2 oz bourbon or rye whiskey*
- *Ice cubes*
- *Lemon twist*
- *Chamomile flower*

Sugar: If using a sugar cube, place it in an Old Fashioned glass and douse with bitters, then muddle until fully dissolved. If using simple syrup, add it directly to the glass along with the bitters.

Chamomile Tea: If using a tea bag, steep it in the bourbon or rye whiskey for 1-2 minutes, and then add the chamomile-infused whiskey to the glass. Otherwise, add the chamomile tea directly to the glass.

Whiskey: If not already added, add the bourbon or rye whiskey to the glass, stirring until fully integrated.

Ice: Add a few ice cubes, stirring gently to chill and dilute the drink slightly.

Garnish: Express the oils of a lemon twist over the drink, and then drop it into the glass, and garnish with a chamomile flower.

Serve: Stir well, and enjoy!

Cherry Old Fashioned

- 1 sugar cube or 1/4 oz simple syrup
- 4-6 dashes of Angostura bitters
- 1/4 oz cherry liqueur or 3-4 fresh cherries, muddled
- 2 oz bourbon or rye whiskey
- Ice cubes
- Orange twist
- Fresh cherry

Sugar: If using a sugar cube, place it in an Old Fashioned glass and douse with bitters, then muddle until fully dissolved. If using simple syrup, add it directly to the glass along with the bitters.

Cherry: If using fresh cherries, add them to the glass and muddle them to release their juice and flavor. Otherwise, add the cherry liqueur directly to the glass, stirring until integrated.

Whiskey: Add the bourbon or rye whiskey to the glass, stirring until fully integrated.

Ice: Add a few ice cubes, stirring gently to chill and dilute the drink slightly.

Garnish: Express the oils of an orange twist over the drink, and then drop it into the glass, and garnish with a fresh cherry.

Serve: Stir well, and enjoy!

Chili Mango Old Fashioned

- *1 sugar cube or 1/4 oz simple syrup*
- *4-6 dashes of Angostura bitters*
- *1/4 oz mango juice or puree*
- *1/8 tsp chili powder or cayenne pepper*
- *2 oz bourbon or rye whiskey*
- *Ice cubes*
- *Mango slice*
- *Chili slice*

Sugar: If using a sugar cube, place it in an Old Fashioned glass and douse with bitters, then muddle until fully dissolved. If using simple syrup, add it directly to the glass along with the bitters.

Mango: Add the mango juice or puree to the glass, stirring until integrated.

Chili Powder: Add the chili powder or cayenne pepper to the glass, stirring to mix.

Whiskey: Add the bourbon or rye whiskey to the glass, stirring until fully integrated.

Ice: Add a few ice cubes, stirring gently to chill and dilute the drink slightly.

Garnish: Garnish with a mango slice and chili slice for a colorful finish.

Serve: Stir well, and enjoy!

Choco-Berry Old Fashioned

- *1 sugar cube or 1/4 oz simple syrup*
- *4-6 dashes of Angostura bitters*
- *1 oz berry puree*
- *1/4 oz chocolate liqueur*
- *2 oz bourbon or rye whiskey*
- *Ice cubes*
- *Orange twist*
- *Fresh berries*

Sugar: If using a sugar cube, place it in an Old Fashioned glass and douse with bitters, then muddle until fully dissolved. If using simple syrup, add it directly to the glass along with the bitters.

Berry Puree: Add the berry puree to the glass, stirring to integrate.

Chocolate Liqueur: Add the chocolate liqueur to the glass, stirring until well mixed.

Whiskey: Add the bourbon or rye whiskey to the glass, stirring until fully integrated.

Ice: Add a few ice cubes, stirring gently to chill and dilute the drink slightly.

Garnish: Express the oils of an orange twist over the drink, and then drop it into the glass, or add both fresh berries and chocolate shavings.

Serve: Stir well, and enjoy!

Chocolate Cherry Old Fashioned

- *1 sugar cube or 1/4 oz simple syrup*
- *4-6 dashes of Angostura bitters*
- *1/4 oz chocolate liqueur*
- *1/4 oz cherry liqueur or 3-4 muddled fresh cherries*
- *2 oz bourbon or rye whiskey*
- *Ice cubes*
- *Orange twist*
- *Cherry or chocolate shavings*

Sugar: If using a sugar cube, place it in an Old Fashioned glass and douse with bitters, then muddle until fully dissolved. If using simple syrup, add it directly to the glass along with the bitters.

Chocolate Liqueur: Add the chocolate liqueur to the glass, stirring until integrated.

Cherry: If using fresh cherries, add them to the glass and muddle them to release their juice and flavor. Otherwise, add the cherry liqueur directly to the glass, stirring until mixed.

Whiskey: Add the bourbon or rye whiskey to the glass, stirring until fully integrated.

Ice: Add a few ice cubes, stirring gently to chill and dilute the drink slightly.

Garnish: Express the oils of an orange twist over the drink, then add both a cherry and chocolate shavings.

Serve: Stir well, and enjoy!

Chocolate Old Fashioned

- I sugar cube or 1/4 oz simple syrup
- 4-6 dashes of Angostura bitters
- 1/4 oz chocolate liqueur or 1/4 tsp unsweetened cocoa powder
- 2 oz bourbon or rye whiskey
- Ice cubes
- Orange twist
- Chocolate shavings or chocolate stick

Sugar: If using a sugar cube, place it in an Old Fashioned glass and douse with bitters, then muddle until fully dissolved. If using simple syrup, add it directly to the glass along with the bitters.

Chocolate: If using cocoa powder, add it to the glass, stirring until dissolved. Otherwise, add the chocolate liqueur, stirring until well mixed.

Whiskey: Add the bourbon or rye whiskey to the glass, stirring until fully integrated.

Ice: Add a few ice cubes, stirring gently to chill and dilute the drink slightly.

Garnish: Express the oils of an orange twist over the drink, and then drop it into the glass, or add chocolate shavings or a chocolate stick.

Serve: Stir well, and enjoy!

Cider Old Fashioned

- ➤ 1 sugar cube or 1/4 oz simple syrup
- ➤ 4-6 dashes of Angostura bitters
- ➤ 1 oz apple cider
- ➤ 2 oz bourbon or rye whiskey
- ➤ Ice cubes
- ➤ Orange twist
- ➤ Apple slice
- ➤ Cinnamon stick

Sugar: If using a sugar cube, place it in an Old Fashioned glass and douse with bitters, then muddle until fully dissolved. If using simple syrup, add it directly to the glass along with the bitters.

Cider: Add the apple cider to the glass, stirring until fully integrated.

Whiskey: Add the bourbon or rye whiskey to the glass, stirring until fully integrated.

Ice: Add a few ice cubes, stirring gently to chill and dilute the drink slightly.

Garnish: Express the oils of an orange twist over the drink, and then drop it into the glass, and add an apple slice and a cinnamon stick.

Serve: Stir well, and enjoy!

Cinnamon Old Fashioned

- *1 sugar cube or 1/4 oz simple syrup*
- *4-6 dashes of Angostura bitters*
- *1/4 oz cinnamon syrup or 1/4 tsp ground cinnamon*
- *2 oz bourbon or rye whiskey*
- *Ice cubes*
- *Orange twist*
- *Cinnamon stick*

Sugar: If using a sugar cube, place it in an Old Fashioned glass and douse with bitters, then muddle until fully dissolved. If using simple syrup, add it directly to the glass along with the bitters.

Cinnamon: If using ground cinnamon, add it to the glass and stir. If using cinnamon syrup, add it to the glass, stirring until integrated.

Whiskey: Add the bourbon or rye whiskey to the glass, stirring until fully integrated.

Ice: Add a few ice cubes, stirring gently to chill and dilute the drink slightly.

Garnish: Express the oils of an orange twist over the drink, and then drop it into the glass, adding a cinnamon stick.

Serve: Stir well, and enjoy!

Clove Vanilla Old Fashioned

- *1 sugar cube or 1/4 oz simple syrup*
- *4-6 dashes of Angostura bitters*
- *1/4 oz vanilla syrup or 1/4 tsp vanilla extract*
- *1/4 tsp ground cloves or 2-3 whole cloves*
- *2 oz bourbon or rye whiskey*
- *Ice cubes*
- *Orange twist*
- *Whole cloves*

Sugar: If using a sugar cube, place it in an Old Fashioned glass and douse with bitters, then muddle until fully dissolved. If using simple syrup, add it directly to the glass along with the bitters.

Vanilla: If using vanilla extract, add it to the glass and stir. If using vanilla syrup, add it to the glass, stirring until integrated.

Cloves: Add the ground cloves or whole cloves to the glass, stirring to mix.

Whiskey: Add the bourbon or rye whiskey to the glass, stirring until fully integrated.

Ice: Add a few ice cubes, stirring gently to chill and dilute the drink slightly.

Garnish: Express the oils of an orange twist over the drink, and then drop it into the glass, adding whole cloves.

Serve: Stir well, and enjoy!

Cocoa Nutmeg Old Fashioned

- I sugar cube or 1/4 oz simple syrup
- 4-6 dashes of Angostura bitters
- 1/4 tsp unsweetened cocoa powder or 1/4 oz chocolate liqueur
- 1/4 tsp ground nutmeg
- 2 oz bourbon or rye whiskey
- Ice cubes
- Orange twist
- Grated nutmeg
- Chocolate shavings

Sugar: If using a sugar cube, place it in an Old Fashioned glass and douse with bitters, then muddle until fully dissolved. If using simple syrup, add it directly to the glass along with the bitters.

Cocoa: If using cocoa powder, add it to the glass and stir until integrated. Otherwise, add the chocolate liqueur directly, stirring to combine.

Nutmeg: Add the ground nutmeg to the glass, stirring until mixed.

Whiskey: Add the bourbon or rye whiskey to the glass, stirring until fully integrated.

Ice: Add a few ice cubes, stirring gently to chill and dilute the drink slightly.

Garnish: Express the oils of an orange twist over the drink, and then drop it into the glass, adding both grated nutmeg and chocolate shavings.

Serve: Stir well, and enjoy!

Coconut Old Fashioned

- I sugar cube or 1/4 oz simple syrup
- 4-6 dashes of Angostura bitters
- 1/4 oz coconut cream or coconut syrup
- 2 oz bourbon or rye whiskey
- Ice cubes
- Orange twist
- Toasted coconut flakes

Sugar: If using a sugar cube, place it in an Old Fashioned glass and douse with bitters, then muddle until fully dissolved. If using simple syrup, add it directly to the glass along with the bitters.

Coconut: Add the coconut cream or syrup to the glass, stirring until integrated.

Whiskey: Add the bourbon or rye whiskey to the glass, stirring until fully integrated.

Ice: Add a few ice cubes, stirring gently to chill and dilute the drink slightly.

Garnish: Express the oils of an orange twist over the drink, and then drop it into the glass, adding toasted coconut flakes.

Serve: Stir well, and enjoy!

Coffee Old Fashioned

- *1 sugar cube or 1/4 oz simple syrup*
- *4-6 dashes of Angostura bitters*
- *1/4 oz coffee liqueur or 1 shot of espresso*
- *2 oz bourbon or rye whiskey*
- *Ice cubes*
- *Orange twist*
- *Coffee beans*

Sugar: If using a sugar cube, place it in an Old Fashioned glass and douse with bitters, then muddle until fully dissolved. If using simple syrup, add it directly to the glass along with the bitters.

Coffee: Add the coffee liqueur or espresso to the glass, stirring until integrated.

Whiskey: Add the bourbon or rye whiskey to the glass, stirring until fully integrated.

Ice: Add a few ice cubes, stirring gently to chill and dilute the drink slightly.

Garnish: Express the oils of an orange twist over the drink, and then drop it into the glass, adding a few coffee beans.

Serve: Stir well, and enjoy!

Cognac Old Fashioned

- I sugar cube or 1/4 oz simple syrup
- 4-6 dashes of Angostura bitters
- 2 oz cognac
- Ice cubes
- Orange twist
- Cherry

Sugar: If using a sugar cube, place it in an Old Fashioned glass and douse with bitters, then muddle until fully dissolved. If using simple syrup, add it directly to the glass along with the bitters.

Cognac: Add the cognac to the glass, stirring until fully integrated.

Ice: Add a few ice cubes, stirring gently to chill and dilute the drink slightly.

Garnish: Express the oils of an orange twist over the drink, and then drop it into the glass, adding a cherry.

Serve: Stir well, and enjoy!

Cumin Old Fashioned

- ➤ 1 sugar cube or 1/4 oz simple syrup
- ➤ 4-6 dashes of Angostura bitters
- ➤ 1/4 tsp ground cumin or 1 cumin seed pod, crushed
- ➤ 2 oz bourbon or rye whiskey
- ➤ Ice cubes
- ➤ Orange twist

Sugar: If using a sugar cube, place it in an Old Fashioned glass and douse with bitters, then muddle until fully dissolved. If using simple syrup, add it directly to the glass along with the bitters.

Cumin: Add the ground cumin or crushed cumin seed pod to the glass, stirring until integrated.

Whiskey: Add the bourbon or rye whiskey to the glass, stirring until fully integrated.

Ice: Add a few ice cubes, stirring gently to chill and dilute the drink slightly.

Garnish: Express the oils of an orange twist over the drink, and then drop it into the glass.

Serve: Stir well, and enjoy!

Drambuie Old Fashioned

- *1 sugar cube or 1/4 oz simple syrup*
- *4-6 dashes of Angostura bitters*
- *1/4 oz Drambuie (a Scotch whisky-based liqueur)*
- *2 oz Scotch whisky*
- *Ice cubes*
- *Orange twist*
- *Lemon twist*

Sugar: If using a sugar cube, place it in an Old Fashioned glass and douse with bitters, then muddle until fully dissolved. If using simple syrup, add it directly to the glass along with the bitters.

Drambuie: Add the Drambuie to the glass, stirring until integrated.

Whisky: Add the Scotch whisky to the glass, stirring until fully integrated.

Ice: Add a few ice cubes, stirring gently to chill and dilute the drink slightly.

Garnish: Express the oils of an orange twist and a lemon twist over the drink, and then drop them into the glass.

Serve: Stir well, and enjoy!

Elderflower Old Fashioned

- *1 sugar cube or 1/4 oz simple syrup*
- *4-6 dashes of Angostura bitters*
- *1/4 oz elderflower liqueur*
- *2 oz bourbon or rye whiskey*
- *Ice cubes*
- *Orange twist*
- *Fresh elderflower*

Sugar: If using a sugar cube, place it in an Old Fashioned glass and douse with bitters, then muddle until fully dissolved. If using simple syrup, add it directly to the glass along with the bitters.

Elderflower Liqueur: Add the elderflower liqueur to the glass, stirring until fully integrated.

Whiskey: Add the bourbon or rye whiskey to the glass, stirring until fully integrated.

Ice: Add a few ice cubes, stirring gently to chill and dilute the drink slightly.

Garnish: Express the oils of an orange twist over the drink, and then drop it into the glass, adding a fresh elderflower.

Serve: Stir well, and enjoy!

Fig Old Fashioned

- I sugar cube or 1/4 oz simple syrup
- 4-6 dashes of Angostura bitters
- 1 oz fig puree or 1/4 oz fig liqueur
- 2 oz bourbon or rye whiskey
- Ice cubes
- Orange twist
- Fig slice

Sugar: If using a sugar cube, place it in an Old Fashioned glass and douse with bitters, then muddle until fully dissolved. If using simple syrup, add it directly to the glass along with the bitters.

Fig: If using fig puree, add it directly to the glass, stirring until integrated. Otherwise, add the fig liqueur, stirring until mixed.

Whiskey: Add the bourbon or rye whiskey to the glass, stirring until fully integrated.

Ice: Add a few ice cubes, stirring gently to chill and dilute the drink slightly.

Garnish: Express the oils of an orange twist over the drink, and then drop it into the glass, adding a fig slice.

Serve: Stir well, and enjoy!

Ginger Old Fashioned

- I sugar cube or 1/4 oz simple syrup
- 4-6 dashes of Angostura bitters
- 1/4 oz ginger syrup or 1 tsp freshly grated ginger
- 2 oz bourbon or rye whiskey
- Ice cubes
- Orange twist
- Candied ginger

Sugar: If using a sugar cube, place it in an Old Fashioned glass and douse with bitters, then muddle until fully dissolved. If using simple syrup, add it directly to the glass along with the bitters.

Ginger: If using grated ginger, add it to the glass, stirring to combine. Otherwise, add the ginger syrup directly, stirring until mixed.

Whiskey: Add the bourbon or rye whiskey to the glass, stirring until fully integrated.

Ice: Add a few ice cubes, stirring gently to chill and dilute the drink slightly.

Garnish: Express the oils of an orange twist over the drink, and then drop it into the glass, adding candied ginger.

Serve: Stir well, and enjoy!

Gingerbread Old Fashioned

- ➤ I sugar cube or 1/4 oz gingerbread syrup
- ➤ 4-6 dashes of Angostura bitters
- ➤ 1/4 tsp ground ginger or 1/4 tsp ground cinnamon
- ➤ 2 oz bourbon or rye whiskey
- ➤ Ice cubes
- ➤ Orange twist
- ➤ Gingerbread cookie piece

Sugar: Place the sugar cube in an Old Fashioned glass and douse with bitters, then muddle until fully dissolved. If using gingerbread syrup, add it directly to the glass along with the bitters.

Spices: Add the ground ginger or ground cinnamon to the glass, stirring until fully integrated.

Whiskey: Add the bourbon or rye whiskey to the glass, stirring until fully integrated.

Ice: Add a few ice cubes, stirring gently to chill and dilute the drink slightly.

Garnish: Express the oils of an orange twist over the drink, and then drop it into the glass, adding a gingerbread cookie piece.

Serve: Stir well, and enjoy!

Grapefruit Old Fashioned

- ➤ 1 sugar cube or 1/4 oz simple syrup
- ➤ 4-6 dashes of Angostura bitters
- ➤ 1 oz grapefruit juice
- ➤ 2 oz bourbon or rye whiskey
- ➤ Ice cubes
- ➤ Orange twist
- ➤ Grapefruit slice

Sugar: Place the sugar cube in an Old Fashioned glass and douse with bitters, then muddle until fully dissolved. If using simple syrup, add it directly to the glass along with the bitters.

Grapefruit Juice: Add the grapefruit juice to the glass, stirring until fully integrated.

Whiskey: Add the bourbon or rye whiskey to the glass, stirring until fully integrated.

Ice: Add a few ice cubes, stirring gently to chill and dilute the drink slightly.

Garnish: Express the oils of an orange twist over the drink, and then drop it into the glass, adding a grapefruit slice.

Serve: Stir well, and enjoy!

Hazelnut Old Fashioned

- 1 sugar cube or 1/4 oz simple syrup
- 4-6 dashes of Angostura bitters
- 1/4 oz hazelnut liqueur or 1 tsp hazelnut syrup
- 2 oz bourbon or rye whiskey
- Ice cubes
- Orange twist
- Crushed hazelnuts

Sugar: Place the sugar cube in an Old Fashioned glass and douse with bitters, then muddle until fully dissolved. If using simple syrup, add it directly to the glass along with the bitters.

Hazelnut: Add the hazelnut liqueur or syrup to the glass, stirring until integrated.

Whiskey: Add the bourbon or rye whiskey to the glass, stirring until fully integrated.

Ice: Add a few ice cubes, stirring gently to chill and dilute the drink slightly.

Garnish: Express the oils of an orange twist over the drink, and then drop it into the glass, adding crushed hazelnuts.

Serve: Stir well, and enjoy!

Hibiscus Old Fashioned

- *1 sugar cube or 1/4 oz simple syrup*
- *4-6 dashes of Angostura bitters*
- *1 oz hibiscus tea or 1/4 oz hibiscus syrup*
- *2 oz bourbon or rye whiskey*
- *Ice cubes*
- *Orange twist*
- *Hibiscus flower or petals*

Sugar: Place the sugar cube in an Old Fashioned glass and douse with bitters, then muddle until fully dissolved. If using simple syrup, add it directly to the glass along with the bitters.

Hibiscus: Add the hibiscus tea or syrup to the glass, stirring until integrated.

Whiskey: Add the bourbon or rye whiskey to the glass, stirring until fully integrated.

Ice: Add a few ice cubes, stirring gently to chill and dilute the drink slightly.

Garnish: Express the oils of an orange twist over the drink, and then drop it into the glass, adding hibiscus flower or petals.

Serve: Stir well, and enjoy!

Honey Old Fashioned

- *1/4 oz honey or 1 sugar cube*
- *4-6 dashes of Angostura bitters*
- *2 oz bourbon or rye whiskey*
- *Ice cubes*
- *Orange twist*
- *Lemon twist*

Sugar: If using a sugar cube, place it in an Old Fashioned glass and douse with bitters, then muddle until fully dissolved. If using honey, add it directly to the glass along with the bitters.

Whiskey: Add the bourbon or rye whiskey to the glass, stirring until fully integrated.

Ice: Add a few ice cubes, stirring gently to chill and dilute the drink slightly.

Garnish: Express the oils of an orange twist and a lemon twist over the drink, and then drop them into the glass.

Serve: Stir well, and enjoy!

Jalapeño Old Fashioned

- *1 sugar cube or 1/4 oz simple syrup*
- *4-6 dashes of Angostura bitters*
- *2-3 slices of jalapeño pepper, muddled*
- *2 oz bourbon or rye whiskey*
- *Ice cubes*
- *Orange twist*
- *Jalapeño slice*

Sugar: If using a sugar cube, place it in an Old Fashioned glass and douse with bitters, then muddle until fully dissolved. If using simple syrup, add it directly to the glass along with the bitters.

Jalapeño: Add the jalapeño slices to the glass and muddle them to release their juice and heat.

Whiskey: Add the bourbon or rye whiskey to the glass, stirring until fully integrated.

Ice: Add a few ice cubes, stirring gently to chill and dilute the drink slightly.

Garnish: Express the oils of an orange twist over the drink, and then drop it into the glass, adding a jalapeño slice.

Serve: Stir well, and enjoy!

Lavender Honey Old Fashioned

- I sugar cube or 1/4 oz honey
- 4-6 dashes of Angostura bitters
- 1/4 oz lavender syrup or 1 tsp dried lavender flowers
- 2 oz bourbon or rye whiskey
- Ice cubes
- Orange twist
- Dried lavender flowers

Sugar: Place the sugar cube in an Old Fashioned glass and douse with bitters, then muddle until fully dissolved. If using honey, add it directly to the glass along with the bitters.

Lavender: If using lavender syrup, add it directly to the glass, stirring until integrated. If using dried lavender flowers, add them directly to the glass.

Whiskey: Add the bourbon or rye whiskey to the glass, stirring until fully integrated.

Ice: Add a few ice cubes, stirring gently to chill and dilute the drink slightly.

Garnish: Express the oils of an orange twist over the drink, and then drop it into the glass, adding dried lavender flowers.

Serve: Stir well, and enjoy!

Lavender Old Fashioned

- I sugar cube or 1/4 oz simple syrup
- 4-6 dashes of Angostura bitters
- 1/4 oz lavender syrup or 1 tsp dried lavender flowers
- 2 oz bourbon or rye whiskey
- Ice cubes
- Orange twist
- Dried lavender flowers

Sugar: Place the sugar cube in an Old Fashioned glass and douse with bitters, then muddle until fully dissolved. If using simple syrup, add it directly to the glass along with the bitters.

Lavender: If using lavender syrup, add it directly to the glass, stirring until integrated. If using dried lavender flowers, add them directly to the glass.

Whiskey: Add the bourbon or rye whiskey to the glass, stirring until fully integrated.

Ice: Add a few ice cubes, stirring gently to chill and dilute the drink slightly.

Garnish: Express the oils of an orange twist over the drink, and then drop it into the glass, adding dried lavender flowers.

Serve: Stir well, and enjoy!

Lemongrass Old Fashioned

- *1 sugar cube or 1/4 oz simple syrup*
- *4-6 dashes of Angostura bitters*
- *1/4 oz lemongrass syrup or 1 tsp finely chopped lemongrass*
- *2 oz bourbon or rye whiskey*
- *Ice cubes*
- *Orange twist*
- *Lemongrass stalk or slices*

Sugar: Place the sugar cube in an Old Fashioned glass and douse with bitters, then muddle until fully dissolved. If using simple syrup, add it directly to the glass along with the bitters.

Lemongrass: If using lemongrass syrup, add it directly to the glass, stirring until integrated. If using chopped lemongrass, add it to the glass.

Whiskey: Add the bourbon or rye whiskey to the glass, stirring until fully integrated.

Ice: Add a few ice cubes, stirring gently to chill and dilute the drink slightly.

Garnish: Express the oils of an orange twist over the drink, and then drop it into the glass, adding a lemongrass stalk or slices.

Serve: Stir well, and enjoy!

Licorice Old Fashioned

- *1 sugar cube or 1/4 oz simple syrup*
- *4-6 dashes of Angostura bitters*
- *1/4 oz licorice liqueur or 1/4 tsp ground anise*
- *2 oz bourbon or rye whiskey*
- *Ice cubes*
- *Orange twist*
- *Star anise*

Sugar: Place the sugar cube in an Old Fashioned glass and douse with bitters, then muddle until fully dissolved. If using simple syrup, add it directly to the glass along with the bitters.

Licorice: If using licorice liqueur, add it directly to the glass, stirring until integrated. If using ground anise, add it directly.

Whiskey: Add the bourbon or rye whiskey to the glass, stirring until fully integrated.

Ice: Add a few ice cubes, stirring gently to chill and dilute the drink slightly.

Garnish: Express the oils of an orange twist over the drink, and then drop it into the glass, adding a star anise.

Serve: Stir well, and enjoy!

Maple Bacon Old Fashioned

- 1 sugar cube or 1/4 oz maple syrup
- 4-6 dashes of Angostura bitters
- 2 oz bourbon or rye whiskey
- Ice cubes
- Orange twist
- Crispy bacon strip

Sugar: Place the sugar cube in an Old Fashioned glass and douse with bitters, then muddle until fully dissolved. If using maple syrup, add it directly to the glass along with the bitters.

Whiskey: Add the bourbon or rye whiskey to the glass, stirring until fully integrated.

Ice: Add a few ice cubes, stirring gently to chill and dilute the drink slightly.

Garnish: Express the oils of an orange twist over the drink, and then drop it into the glass, adding a crispy bacon strip.

Serve: Stir well, and enjoy!

Maple Old Fashioned

- ➤ 1 sugar cube or 1/4 oz maple syrup
- ➤ 4-6 dashes of Angostura bitters
- ➤ 2 oz bourbon or rye whiskey
- ➤ Ice cubes
- ➤ Orange twist
- ➤ Cherry

Sugar: Place the sugar cube in an Old Fashioned glass and douse with bitters, then muddle until fully dissolved. If using maple syrup, add it directly to the glass along with the bitters.

Whiskey: Add the bourbon or rye whiskey to the glass, stirring until fully integrated.

Ice: Add a few ice cubes, stirring gently to chill and dilute the drink slightly.

Garnish: Express the oils of an orange twist over the drink, and then drop it into the glass, adding a cherry.

Serve: Stir well, and enjoy!

Maple Walnut Old Fashioned

- I sugar cube or 1/4 oz maple syrup
- 4-6 dashes of Angostura bitters
- 1/4 oz walnut liqueur or 1 tbsp crushed walnuts
- 2 oz bourbon or rye whiskey
- Ice cubes
- Orange twist
- Crushed walnuts

Sugar: Place the sugar cube in an Old Fashioned glass and douse with bitters, then muddle until fully dissolved. If using maple syrup, add it directly to the glass along with the bitters.

Walnut: If using walnut liqueur, add it directly to the glass, stirring until integrated. If using crushed walnuts, add them directly to the glass.

Whiskey: Add the bourbon or rye whiskey to the glass, stirring until fully integrated.

Ice: Add a few ice cubes, stirring gently to chill and dilute the drink slightly.

Garnish: Express the oils of an orange twist over the drink, and then drop it into the glass, adding crushed walnuts.

Serve: Stir well, and enjoy!

Matcha Old Fashioned

- I sugar cube or 1/4 oz simple syrup
- 4-6 dashes of Angostura bitters
- 1/4 tsp matcha powder or 1 oz matcha tea
- 2 oz bourbon or rye whiskey
- Ice cubes
- Orange twist
- Matcha powder or leaves

Sugar: Place the sugar cube in an Old Fashioned glass and douse with bitters, then muddle until fully dissolved. If using simple syrup, add it directly to the glass along with the bitters.

Matcha: If using matcha powder, add it directly to the glass, stirring until integrated. If using matcha tea, add it directly to the glass.

Whiskey: Add the bourbon or rye whiskey to the glass, stirring until fully integrated.

Ice: Add a few ice cubes, stirring gently to chill and dilute the drink slightly.

Garnish: Express the oils of an orange twist over the drink, and then drop it into the glass, adding a sprinkle of matcha powder or some matcha leaves.

Serve: Stir well, and enjoy!

Mezcal Old Fashioned

- ➤ 1 sugar cube or 1/4 oz simple syrup
- ➤ 4-6 dashes of Angostura bitters
- ➤ 2 oz mezcal
- ➤ Ice cubes
- ➤ Orange twist
- ➤ Lemon twist

Sugar: Place the sugar cube in an Old Fashioned glass and douse with bitters, then muddle until fully dissolved. If using simple syrup, add it directly to the glass along with the bitters.

Mezcal: Add the mezcal to the glass, stirring until fully integrated.

Ice: Add a few ice cubes, stirring gently to chill and dilute the drink slightly.

Garnish: Express the oils of an orange twist and a lemon twist over the drink, and then drop them into the glass.

Serve: Stir well, and enjoy!

Mint Old Fashioned

➤ *1 sugar cube or 1/4 oz simple syrup*
➤ *4-6 dashes of Angostura bitters*
➤ *1-2 fresh mint leaves, muddled*
➤ *2 oz bourbon or rye whiskey*
➤ *Ice cubes*
➤ *Orange twist*
➤ *Mint sprig*

Sugar: Place the sugar cube in an Old Fashioned glass and douse with bitters, then muddle until fully dissolved. If using simple syrup, add it directly to the glass along with the bitters.

Mint: Add the fresh mint leaves to the glass and muddle them to release their flavor.

Whiskey: Add the bourbon or rye whiskey to the glass, stirring until fully integrated.

Ice: Add a few ice cubes, stirring gently to chill and dilute the drink slightly.

Garnish: Express the oils of an orange twist over the drink, and then drop it into the glass, adding a mint sprig.

Serve: Stir well, and enjoy!

Mocha Old Fashioned

- *1 sugar cube or 1/4 oz simple syrup*
- *4-6 dashes of Angostura bitters*
- *1/4 oz coffee liqueur or 1 shot espresso*
- *1/4 oz chocolate liqueur or 1/4 tsp cocoa powder*
- *2 oz bourbon or rye whiskey*
- *Ice cubes*
- *Orange twist*
- *Chocolate shavings*
- *Coffee beans*

Sugar: Place the sugar cube in an Old Fashioned glass and douse with bitters, then muddle until fully dissolved. If using simple syrup, add it directly to the glass along with the bitters.

Mocha: Add the coffee liqueur or espresso, and the chocolate liqueur or cocoa powder to the glass, stirring until integrated.

Whiskey: Add the bourbon or rye whiskey to the glass, stirring until fully integrated.

Ice: Add a few ice cubes, stirring gently to chill and dilute the drink slightly.

Garnish: Express the oils of an orange twist over the drink, and then drop it into the glass, adding chocolate shavings and coffee beans.

Serve: Stir well, and enjoy!

Nutmeg Old Fashioned

- I sugar cube or 1/4 oz simple syrup
- 4-6 dashes of Angostura bitters
- 1/4 tsp ground nutmeg
- 2 oz bourbon or rye whiskey
- Ice cubes
- Orange twist
- Grated nutmeg

Sugar: Place the sugar cube in an Old Fashioned glass and douse with bitters, then muddle until fully dissolved. If using simple syrup, add it directly to the glass along with the bitters.

Nutmeg: Add the ground nutmeg to the glass, stirring until integrated.

Whiskey: Add the bourbon or rye whiskey to the glass, stirring until fully integrated.

Ice: Add a few ice cubes, stirring gently to chill and dilute the drink slightly.

Garnish: Express the oils of an orange twist over the drink, and then drop it into the glass, adding grated nutmeg.

Serve: Stir well, and enjoy!

Orange Old Fashioned

- *1 sugar cube or 1/4 oz simple syrup*
- *4-6 dashes of Angostura bitters*
- *1/2 oz orange juice*
- *2 oz bourbon or rye whiskey*
- *Ice cubes*
- *Orange twist*
- *Orange slice*

Sugar: Place the sugar cube in an Old Fashioned glass and douse with bitters, then muddle until fully dissolved. If using simple syrup, add it directly to the glass along with the bitters.

Orange Juice: Add the orange juice to the glass, stirring until fully integrated.

Whiskey: Add the bourbon or rye whiskey to the glass, stirring until fully integrated.

Ice: Add a few ice cubes, stirring gently to chill and dilute the drink slightly.

Garnish: Express the oils of an orange twist over the drink, and then drop it into the glass, adding an orange slice.

Serve: Stir well, and enjoy!

Oregano Old Fashioned

- *1 sugar cube or 1/4 oz simple syrup*
- *4-6 dashes of Angostura bitters*
- *1 tsp fresh oregano, muddled or 1/4 oz oregano syrup*
- *2 oz bourbon or rye whiskey*
- *Ice cubes*
- *Orange twist*
- *Oregano sprig*

Sugar: Place the sugar cube in an Old Fashioned glass and douse with bitters, then muddle until fully dissolved. If using simple syrup, add it directly to the glass along with the bitters.

Oregano: If using fresh oregano, add it to the glass and muddle to release its flavor. If using oregano syrup, add it directly to the glass, stirring until integrated.

Whiskey: Add the bourbon or rye whiskey to the glass, stirring until fully integrated.

Ice: Add a few ice cubes, stirring gently to chill and dilute the drink slightly.

Garnish: Express the oils of an orange twist over the drink, and then drop it into the glass, adding an oregano sprig.

Serve: Stir well, and enjoy!

Peach Old Fashioned

- *1 sugar cube or 1/4 oz simple syrup*
- *4–6 dashes of Angostura bitters*
- *1/4 oz peach liqueur or 1 oz peach puree*
- *2 oz bourbon or rye whiskey*
- *Ice cubes*
- *Orange twist*
- *Peach slice*

Sugar: Place the sugar cube in an Old Fashioned glass and douse with bitters, then muddle until fully dissolved. If using simple syrup, add it directly to the glass along with the bitters.

Peach: If using peach puree, add it directly to the glass, stirring until integrated. If using peach liqueur, add it directly to the glass.

Whiskey: Add the bourbon or rye whiskey to the glass, stirring until fully integrated.

Ice: Add a few ice cubes, stirring gently to chill and dilute the drink slightly.

Garnish: Express the oils of an orange twist over the drink, and then drop it into the glass, adding a peach slice.

Serve: Stir well, and enjoy!

Pear Old Fashioned

- *1 sugar cube or 1/4 oz simple syrup*
- *4-6 dashes of Angostura bitters*
- *1/4 oz pear liqueur or 1 oz pear puree*
- *2 oz bourbon or rye whiskey*
- *Ice cubes*
- *Orange twist*
- *Pear slice*

Sugar: Place the sugar cube in an Old Fashioned glass and douse with bitters, then muddle until fully dissolved. If using simple syrup, add it directly to the glass along with the bitters.

Pear: If using pear puree, add it directly to the glass, stirring until integrated. If using pear liqueur, add it directly to the glass.

Whiskey: Add the bourbon or rye whiskey to the glass, stirring until fully integrated.

Ice: Add a few ice cubes, stirring gently to chill and dilute the drink slightly.

Garnish: Express the oils of an orange twist over the drink, and then drop it into the glass, adding a pear slice.

Serve: Stir well, and enjoy!

Peppermint Old Fashioned

- 1 sugar cube or 1/4 oz simple syrup
- 4-6 dashes of Angostura bitters
- 1/4 oz peppermint liqueur or 1/2 tsp peppermint extract
- 2 oz bourbon or rye whiskey
- Ice cubes
- Orange twist
- Mint sprig

Sugar: Place the sugar cube in an Old Fashioned glass and douse with bitters, then muddle until fully dissolved. If using simple syrup, add it directly to the glass along with the bitters.

Peppermint: Add the peppermint liqueur or extract to the glass, stirring until integrated.

Whiskey: Add the bourbon or rye whiskey to the glass, stirring until fully integrated.

Ice: Add a few ice cubes, stirring gently to chill and dilute the drink slightly.

Garnish: Express the oils of an orange twist over the drink, and then drop it into the glass, adding a mint sprig.

Serve: Stir well, and enjoy!

Pine Nut Old Fashioned

- *1 sugar cube or 1/4 oz simple syrup*
- *4-6 dashes of Angostura bitters*
- *1/4 oz pine nut liqueur or 1 tbsp crushed pine nuts*
- *2 oz bourbon or rye whiskey*
- *Ice cubes*
- *Orange twist*
- *Crushed pine nuts*

Sugar: Place the sugar cube in an Old Fashioned glass and douse with bitters, then muddle until fully dissolved. If using simple syrup, add it directly to the glass along with the bitters.

Pine Nut: If using liqueur, add it directly to the glass, stirring until integrated. If using crushed pine nuts, add them directly to the glass.

Whiskey: Add the bourbon or rye whiskey to the glass, stirring until fully integrated.

Ice: Add a few ice cubes, stirring gently to chill and dilute the drink slightly.

Garnish: Express the oils of an orange twist over the drink, and then drop it into the glass, adding crushed pine nuts.

Serve: Stir well, and enjoy!

Pineapple Old Fashioned

- I sugar cube or 1/4 oz simple syrup
- 4-6 dashes of Angostura bitters
- I oz pineapple juice or 1/4 oz pineapple liqueur
- 2 oz bourbon or rye whiskey
- Ice cubes
- Orange twist
- Pineapple slice

Sugar: Place the sugar cube in an Old Fashioned glass and douse with bitters, then muddle until fully dissolved. If using simple syrup, add it directly to the glass along with the bitters.

Pineapple: If using pineapple juice or liqueur, add it directly to the glass, stirring until integrated.

Whiskey: Add the bourbon or rye whiskey to the glass, stirring until fully integrated.

Ice: Add a few ice cubes, stirring gently to chill and dilute the drink slightly.

Garnish: Express the oils of an orange twist over the drink, and then drop it into the glass, adding a pineapple slice.

Serve: Stir well, and enjoy!

Pomegranate Old Fashioned

- I sugar cube or 1/4 oz simple syrup
- 4-6 dashes of Angostura bitters
- I oz pomegranate juice or 1/4 oz pomegranate syrup
- 2 oz bourbon or rye whiskey
- Ice cubes
- Orange twist
- Pomegranate seeds

Sugar: Place the sugar cube in an Old Fashioned glass and douse with bitters, then muddle until fully dissolved. If using simple syrup, add it directly to the glass along with the bitters.

Pomegranate: If using pomegranate juice or syrup, add it directly to the glass, stirring until integrated.

Whiskey: Add the bourbon or rye whiskey to the glass, stirring until fully integrated.

Ice: Add a few ice cubes, stirring gently to chill and dilute the drink slightly.

Garnish: Express the oils of an orange twist over the drink, and then drop it into the glass, adding pomegranate seeds.

Serve: Stir well, and enjoy!

Pumpkin Old Fashioned

- ➤ *1 sugar cube or 1/4 oz simple syrup*
- ➤ *4-6 dashes of Angostura bitters*
- ➤ *1 oz pumpkin puree*
- ➤ *1/4 tsp pumpkin spice blend*
- ➤ *2 oz bourbon or rye whiskey*
- ➤ *Ice cubes*
- ➤ *Orange twist*
- ➤ *Cinnamon stick*

Sugar: Place the sugar cube in an Old Fashioned glass and douse with bitters, then muddle until fully dissolved. If using simple syrup, add it directly to the glass along with the bitters.

Pumpkin: Add the pumpkin puree to the glass, stirring until integrated. Then add the pumpkin spice blend.

Whiskey: Add the bourbon or rye whiskey to the glass, stirring until fully integrated.

Ice: Add a few ice cubes, stirring gently to chill and dilute the drink slightly.

Garnish: Express the oils of an orange twist over the drink, and then drop it into the glass, adding a cinnamon stick.

Serve: Stir well, and enjoy!

Raspberry Old Fashioned

➤ *1 sugar cube or 1/4 oz simple syrup*
➤ *4-6 dashes of Angostura bitters*
➤ *4-6 fresh raspberries, muddled*
➤ *2 oz bourbon or rye whiskey*
➤ *Ice cubes*
➤ *Orange twist*
➤ *Fresh raspberries*

Sugar: Place the sugar cube in an Old Fashioned glass and douse with bitters, then muddle until fully dissolved. If using simple syrup, add it directly to the glass along with the bitters.

Raspberries: Add the fresh raspberries to the glass and muddle them to release their juice and flavor.

Whiskey: Add the bourbon or rye whiskey to the glass, stirring until fully integrated.

Ice: Add a few ice cubes, stirring gently to chill and dilute the drink slightly.

Garnish: Express the oils of an orange twist over the drink, and then drop it into the glass, adding fresh raspberries.

Serve: Stir well, and enjoy!

Rose Old Fashioned

- *1 sugar cube or 1/4 oz simple syrup*
- *4-6 dashes of Angostura bitters*
- *1/4 oz rose syrup or 1 tsp dried rose petals*
- *2 oz bourbon or rye whiskey*
- *Ice cubes*
- *Orange twist*
- *Dried rose petals*

Sugar: Place the sugar cube in an Old Fashioned glass and douse with bitters, then muddle until fully dissolved. If using simple syrup, add it directly to the glass along with the bitters.

Rose: If using rose syrup, add it directly to the glass, stirring until integrated. If using dried rose petals, add them directly.

Whiskey: Add the bourbon or rye whiskey to the glass, stirring until fully integrated.

Ice: Add a few ice cubes, stirring gently to chill and dilute the drink slightly.

Garnish: Express the oils of an orange twist over the drink, and then drop it into the glass, adding dried rose petals.

Serve: Stir well, and enjoy!

Rosemary Old Fashioned

- *1 sugar cube or 1/4 oz simple syrup*
- *4-6 dashes of Angostura bitters*
- *1-2 sprigs of rosemary, muddled*
- *2 oz bourbon or rye whiskey*
- *Ice cubes*
- *Orange twist*
- *Fresh rosemary sprig*

Sugar: Place the sugar cube in an Old Fashioned glass and douse with bitters, then muddle until fully dissolved. If using simple syrup, add it directly to the glass along with the bitters.

Rosemary: Add the rosemary sprigs to the glass and muddle them to release their flavor.

Whiskey: Add the bourbon or rye whiskey to the glass, stirring until fully integrated.

Ice: Add a few ice cubes, stirring gently to chill and dilute the drink slightly.

Garnish: Express the oils of an orange twist over the drink, and then drop it into the glass, adding a fresh rosemary sprig.

Serve: Stir well, and enjoy!

Rum Old Fashioned

- ➤ *1 sugar cube or 1/4 oz simple syrup*
- ➤ *4-6 dashes of Angostura bitters*
- ➤ *2 oz dark rum*
- ➤ *Ice cubes*
- ➤ *Orange twist*
- ➤ *Lime twist*

Sugar: Place the sugar cube in an Old Fashioned glass and douse with bitters, then muddle until fully dissolved. If using simple syrup, add it directly to the glass along with the bitters.

Rum: Add the dark rum to the glass, stirring until fully integrated.

Ice: Add a few ice cubes, stirring gently to chill and dilute the drink slightly.

Garnish: Express the oils of an orange twist and a lime twist over the drink, and then drop them into the glass.

Serve: Stir well, and enjoy!

Rye Old Fashioned

- 1 sugar cube or 1/4 oz simple syrup
- 4-6 dashes of Angostura bitters
- 2 oz rye whiskey
- Ice cubes
- Orange twist
- Cherry

Sugar: Place the sugar cube in an Old Fashioned glass and douse with bitters, then muddle until fully dissolved. If using simple syrup, add it directly to the glass along with the bitters.

Whiskey: Add the rye whiskey to the glass, stirring until fully integrated.

Ice: Add a few ice cubes, stirring gently to chill and dilute the drink slightly.

Garnish: Express the oils of an orange twist over the drink, and then drop it into the glass, adding a cherry.

Serve: Stir well, and enjoy!

Saffron Old Fashioned

- ➤ *1 sugar cube or 1/4 oz simple syrup*
- ➤ *4-6 dashes of Angostura bitters*
- ➤ *1 pinch of saffron threads, crushed or 1/4 oz saffron syrup*
- ➤ *2 oz bourbon or rye whiskey*
- ➤ *Ice cubes*
- ➤ *Orange twist*
- ➤ *Saffron threads*

Sugar: Place the sugar cube in an Old Fashioned glass and douse with bitters, then muddle until fully dissolved. If using simple syrup, add it directly to the glass along with the bitters.

Saffron: If using saffron threads, crush them and add them to the glass, stirring until integrated. If using saffron syrup, add it directly to the glass.

Whiskey: Add the bourbon or rye whiskey to the glass, stirring until fully integrated.

Ice: Add a few ice cubes, stirring gently to chill and dilute the drink slightly.

Garnish: Express the oils of an orange twist over the drink, and then drop it into the glass, adding saffron threads.

Serve: Stir well, and enjoy!

Sarsaparilla Old Fashioned

- *1 sugar cube or 1/4 oz simple syrup*
- *4-6 dashes of Angostura bitters*
- *1/4 oz sarsaparilla syrup or 1 tsp ground sarsaparilla root*
- *2 oz bourbon or rye whiskey*
- *Ice cubes*
- *Orange twist*
- *Sarsaparilla root*

Sugar: Place the sugar cube in an Old Fashioned glass and douse with bitters, then muddle until fully dissolved. If using simple syrup, add it directly to the glass along with the bitters.

Sarsaparilla: If using syrup, add it directly to the glass, stirring until integrated. If using ground sarsaparilla root, add it directly to the glass.

Whiskey: Add the bourbon or rye whiskey to the glass, stirring until fully integrated.

Ice: Add a few ice cubes, stirring gently to chill and dilute the drink slightly.

Garnish: Express the oils of an orange twist over the drink, and then drop it into the glass, adding sarsaparilla root.

Serve: Stir well, and enjoy!

Smoked Cherry Old Fashioned

- ➤ *1 sugar cube or 1/4 oz simple syrup*
- ➤ *4-6 dashes of Angostura bitters*
- ➤ *1 oz cherry liqueur or 3-4 muddled cherries*
- ➤ *2 oz bourbon or rye whiskey*
- ➤ *Ice cubes*
- ➤ *Orange twist*
- ➤ *Smoked cherry*

Sugar: Place the sugar cube in an Old Fashioned glass and douse with bitters, then muddle until fully dissolved. If using simple syrup, add it directly to the glass along with the bitters.

Cherry: If using muddled cherries, add them to the glass and muddle to release their juice and flavor. Otherwise, add the cherry liqueur directly.

Whiskey: Add the bourbon or rye whiskey to the glass, stirring until fully integrated.

Ice: Add a few ice cubes, stirring gently to chill and dilute the drink slightly.

Garnish: Express the oils of an orange twist over the drink, and then drop it into the glass, adding a smoked cherry.

Serve: Stir well, and enjoy!

Smoked Old Fashioned

➤ 1 sugar cube or 1/4 oz simple syrup
➤ 4-6 dashes of Angostura bitters
➤ 2 oz bourbon or rye whiskey
➤ Ice cubes
➤ Orange twist
➤ Smoked rosemary sprig

Sugar: Place the sugar cube in an Old Fashioned glass and douse with bitters, then muddle until fully dissolved. If using simple syrup, add it directly to the glass along with the bitters.

Whiskey: Add the bourbon or rye whiskey to the glass, stirring until fully integrated.

Ice: Add a few ice cubes, stirring gently to chill and dilute the drink slightly.

Garnish: Express the oils of an orange twist over the drink, and then drop it into the glass, adding a smoked rosemary sprig.

Serve: Stir well, and enjoy!

Smoky Agave Old Fashioned

- ➢ 1 sugar cube or 1/4 oz agave syrup
- ➢ 4-6 dashes of Angostura bitters
- ➢ 2 oz mezcal
- ➢ Ice cubes
- ➢ Orange twist
- ➢ Lemon twist

Sugar: Place the sugar cube in an Old Fashioned glass and douse with bitters, then muddle until fully dissolved. If using agave syrup, add it directly to the glass along with the bitters.

Mezcal: Add the mezcal to the glass, stirring until fully integrated.

Ice: Add a few ice cubes, stirring gently to chill and dilute the drink slightly.

Garnish: Express the oils of an orange twist and a lemon twist over the drink, and then drop them into the glass.

Serve: Stir well, and enjoy!

Smoky Maple Old Fashioned

- 1 sugar cube or 1/4 oz maple syrup
- 4-6 dashes of Angostura bitters
- 2 oz bourbon or rye whiskey
- Ice cubes
- Orange twist
- Cinnamon stick

Sugar: Place the sugar cube in an Old Fashioned glass and douse with bitters, then muddle until fully dissolved. If using maple syrup, add it directly to the glass along with the bitters.

Whiskey: Add the bourbon or rye whiskey to the glass, stirring until fully integrated.

Ice: Add a few ice cubes, stirring gently to chill and dilute the drink slightly.

Garnish: Express the oils of an orange twist over the drink, and then drop it into the glass, adding a cinnamon stick.

Serve: Stir well, and enjoy!

Smoky Mezcal Old Fashioned

- ➤ *1 sugar cube or 1/4 oz simple syrup*
- ➤ *4–6 dashes of Angostura bitters*
- ➤ *2 oz mezcal*
- ➤ *Ice cubes*
- ➤ *Orange twist*
- ➤ *Lemon twist*

Sugar: Place the sugar cube in an Old Fashioned glass and douse with bitters, then muddle until fully dissolved. If using simple syrup, add it directly to the glass along with the bitters.

Mezcal: Add the mezcal to the glass, stirring until fully integrated.

Ice: Add a few ice cubes, stirring gently to chill and dilute the drink slightly.

Garnish: Express the oils of an orange twist and a lemon twist over the drink, and then drop them into the glass.

Serve: Stir well, and enjoy!

Spiced Old Fashioned

➤ *1 sugar cube or 1/4 oz simple syrup*
➤ *4-6 dashes of Angostura bitters*
➤ *1/4 tsp pumpkin spice blend or 1/4 oz spiced syrup*
➤ *2 oz bourbon or rye whiskey*
➤ *Ice cubes*
➤ *Orange twist*
➤ *Cinnamon stick*

Sugar: Place the sugar cube in an Old Fashioned glass and douse with bitters, then muddle until fully dissolved. If using simple syrup, add it directly to the glass along with the bitters.

Spices: If using pumpkin spice blend, add it to the glass, stirring to integrate. If using spiced syrup, add it directly.

Whiskey: Add the bourbon or rye whiskey to the glass, stirring until fully integrated.

Ice: Add a few ice cubes, stirring gently to chill and dilute the drink slightly.

Garnish: Express the oils of an orange twist over the drink, and then drop it into the glass, adding a cinnamon stick.

Serve: Stir well, and enjoy!

Spicy Old Fashioned

- *1 sugar cube or 1/4 oz simple syrup*
- *4-6 dashes of Angostura bitters*
- *1/4 tsp cayenne pepper or 1/2 tsp hot sauce*
- *2 oz bourbon or rye whiskey*
- *Ice cubes*
- *Orange twist*
- *Jalapeño slice*

Sugar: Place the sugar cube in an Old Fashioned glass and douse with bitters, then muddle until fully dissolved. If using simple syrup, add it directly to the glass along with the bitters.

Spicy Element: If using cayenne pepper, add it directly to the glass, stirring to integrate. If using hot sauce, add it directly.

Whiskey: Add the bourbon or rye whiskey to the glass, stirring until fully integrated.

Ice: Add a few ice cubes, stirring gently to chill and dilute the drink slightly.

Garnish: Express the oils of an orange twist over the drink, and then drop it into the glass, adding a jalapeño slice.

Serve: Stir well, and enjoy!

Sriracha Old Fashioned

- 1 sugar cube or 1/4 oz simple syrup
- 4-6 dashes of Angostura bitters
- 1/4 tsp sriracha or 1/2 tsp chili paste
- 2 oz bourbon or rye whiskey
- Ice cubes
- Orange twist
- Chili slice

Sugar: Place the sugar cube in an Old Fashioned glass and douse with bitters, then muddle until fully dissolved. If using simple syrup, add it directly to the glass along with the bitters.

Sriracha: Add the sriracha or chili paste to the glass, stirring until fully integrated.

Whiskey: Add the bourbon or rye whiskey to the glass, stirring until fully integrated.

Ice: Add a few ice cubes, stirring gently to chill and dilute the drink slightly.

Garnish: Express the oils of an orange twist over the drink, and then drop it into the glass, adding a chili slice.

Serve: Stir well, and enjoy!

Szechuan Peppercorn Old Fashioned

- *1 sugar cube or 1/4 oz simple syrup*
- *4-6 dashes of Angostura bitters*
- *1/4 tsp crushed Szechuan peppercorns*
- *2 oz bourbon or rye whiskey*
- *Ice cubes*
- *Orange twist*
- *Szechuan peppercorns*

Sugar: Place the sugar cube in an Old Fashioned glass and douse with bitters, then muddle until fully dissolved. If using simple syrup, add it directly to the glass along with the bitters.

Peppercorns: Add the crushed Szechuan peppercorns to the glass, stirring until integrated.

Whiskey: Add the bourbon or rye whiskey to the glass, stirring until fully integrated.

Ice: Add a few ice cubes, stirring gently to chill and dilute the drink slightly.

Garnish: Express the oils of an orange twist over the drink, and then drop it into the glass, adding Szechuan peppercorns.

Serve: Stir well, and enjoy!

Tequila Old Fashioned

- ➤ *1 sugar cube or 1/4 oz agave syrup*
- ➤ *4-6 dashes of Angostura bitters*
- ➤ *2 oz tequila (preferably aged or reposado)*
- ➤ *Ice cubes*
- ➤ *Orange twist*
- ➤ *Lime wedge*

Sugar: Place the sugar cube in an Old Fashioned glass and douse with bitters, then muddle until fully dissolved. If using agave syrup, add it directly to the glass along with the bitters.

Tequila: Add the tequila to the glass, stirring until fully integrated.

Ice: Add a few ice cubes, stirring gently to chill and dilute the drink slightly.

Garnish: Express the oils of an orange twist over the drink, and then drop it into the glass, adding a lime wedge.

Serve: Stir well, and enjoy!

Thyme Old Fashioned

- *1 sugar cube or 1/4 oz simple syrup*
- *4-6 dashes of Angostura bitters*
- *1 tsp fresh thyme, muddled*
- *2 oz bourbon or rye whiskey*
- *Ice cubes*
- *Orange twist*
- *Thyme sprig*

Sugar: Place the sugar cube in an Old Fashioned glass and douse with bitters, then muddle until fully dissolved. If using simple syrup, add it directly to the glass along with the bitters.

Thyme: Add the fresh thyme to the glass and muddle it to release its flavor.

Whiskey: Add the bourbon or rye whiskey to the glass, stirring until fully integrated.

Ice: Add a few ice cubes, stirring gently to chill and dilute the drink slightly.

Garnish: Express the oils of an orange twist over the drink, and then drop it into the glass, adding a thyme sprig.

Serve: Stir well, and enjoy!

Tomato Old Fashioned

- *1 sugar cube or 1/4 oz simple syrup*
- *4-6 dashes of Angostura bitters*
- *1 oz tomato juice or 1 tbsp tomato puree*
- *2 oz bourbon or rye whiskey*
- *Ice cubes*
- *Orange twist*
- *Cherry tomato*

Sugar: Place the sugar cube in an Old Fashioned glass and douse with bitters, then muddle until fully dissolved. If using simple syrup, add it directly to the glass along with the bitters.

Tomato: If using tomato juice, add it directly to the glass, stirring until integrated. If using tomato puree, add it directly to the glass.

Whiskey: Add the bourbon or rye whiskey to the glass, stirring until fully integrated.

Ice: Add a few ice cubes, stirring gently to chill and dilute the drink slightly.

Garnish: Express the oils of an orange twist over the drink, and then drop it into the glass, adding a cherry tomato.

Serve: Stir well, and enjoy!

Tonic Old Fashioned

- ➤ 1 sugar cube or 1/4 oz simple syrup
- ➤ 4-6 dashes of Angostura bitters
- ➤ 1 oz tonic water
- ➤ 2 oz bourbon or rye whiskey
- ➤ Ice cubes
- ➤ Orange twist
- ➤ Lime wedge

Sugar: Place the sugar cube in an Old Fashioned glass and douse with bitters, then muddle until fully dissolved. If using simple syrup, add it directly to the glass along with the bitters.

Tonic Water: Add the tonic water to the glass, stirring until fully integrated.

Whiskey: Add the bourbon or rye whiskey to the glass, stirring until fully integrated.

Ice: Add a few ice cubes, stirring gently to chill and dilute the drink slightly.

Garnish: Express the oils of an orange twist over the drink, and then drop it into the glass, adding a lime wedge.

Serve: Stir well, and enjoy!

Tropical Old Fashioned

- *1 sugar cube or 1/4 oz simple syrup*
- *4-6 dashes of Angostura bitters*
- *1 oz tropical juice blend (such as pineapple, mango, or passionfruit)*
- *2 oz bourbon or rye whiskey*
- *Ice cubes*
- *Orange twist*
- *Tropical fruit slice*

Sugar: Place the sugar cube in an Old Fashioned glass and douse with bitters, then muddle until fully dissolved. If using simple syrup, add it directly to the glass along with the bitters.

Tropical Juice: Add the tropical juice blend to the glass, stirring until integrated.

Whiskey: Add the bourbon or rye whiskey to the glass, stirring until fully integrated.

Ice: Add a few ice cubes, stirring gently to chill and dilute the drink slightly.

Garnish: Express the oils of an orange twist over the drink, and then drop it into the glass, adding a tropical fruit slice.

Serve: Stir well, and enjoy!

Truffle Old Fashioned

- ➤ *1 sugar cube or 1/4 oz simple syrup*
- ➤ *4-6 dashes of Angostura bitters*
- ➤ *1/4 tsp truffle oil or 1/4 oz truffle liqueur*
- ➤ *2 oz bourbon or rye whiskey*
- ➤ *Ice cubes*
- ➤ *Orange twist*
- ➤ *Truffle shavings*

Sugar: Place the sugar cube in an Old Fashioned glass and douse with bitters, then muddle until fully dissolved. If using simple syrup, add it directly to the glass along with the bitters.

Truffle: Add the truffle oil or liqueur to the glass, stirring until integrated.

Whiskey: Add the bourbon or rye whiskey to the glass, stirring until fully integrated.

Ice: Add a few ice cubes, stirring gently to chill and dilute the drink slightly.

Garnish: Express the oils of an orange twist over the drink, and then drop it into the glass, adding truffle shavings.

Serve: Stir well, and enjoy!

Turmeric Old Fashioned

- ➤ *1 sugar cube or 1/4 oz simple syrup*
- ➤ *4-6 dashes of Angostura bitters*
- ➤ *1/4 tsp ground turmeric or 1 oz turmeric tea*
- ➤ *2 oz bourbon or rye whiskey*
- ➤ *Ice cubes*
- ➤ *Orange twist*
- ➤ *Grated turmeric*

Sugar: Place the sugar cube in an Old Fashioned glass and douse with bitters, then muddle until fully dissolved. If using simple syrup, add it directly to the glass along with the bitters.

Turmeric: If using ground turmeric, add it directly to the glass, stirring until integrated. If using turmeric tea, add it directly.

Whiskey: Add the bourbon or rye whiskey to the glass, stirring until fully integrated.

Ice: Add a few ice cubes, stirring gently to chill and dilute the drink slightly.

Garnish: Express the oils of an orange twist over the drink, and then drop it into the glass, adding grated turmeric.

Serve: Stir well, and enjoy!

Vanilla Old Fashioned

- *1 sugar cube or 1/4 oz vanilla syrup*
- *4-6 dashes of Angostura bitters*
- *2 oz bourbon or rye whiskey*
- *Ice cubes*
- *Orange twist*
- *Vanilla bean pod*

Sugar: Place the sugar cube in an Old Fashioned glass and douse with bitters, then muddle until fully dissolved. If using vanilla syrup, add it directly to the glass along with the bitters.

Whiskey: Add the bourbon or rye whiskey to the glass, stirring until fully integrated.

Ice: Add a few ice cubes, stirring gently to chill and dilute the drink slightly.

Garnish: Express the oils of an orange twist over the drink, and then drop it into the glass, adding a vanilla bean pod.

Serve: Stir well, and enjoy!

Walnut Old Fashioned

- *1 sugar cube or 1/4 oz walnut syrup*
- *4-6 dashes of Angostura bitters*
- *2 oz bourbon or rye whiskey*
- *Ice cubes*
- *Orange twist*
- *Crushed walnuts*

Sugar: Place the sugar cube in an Old Fashioned glass and douse with bitters, then muddle until fully dissolved. If using walnut syrup, add it directly to the glass along with the bitters.

Whiskey: Add the bourbon or rye whiskey to the glass, stirring until fully integrated.

Ice: Add a few ice cubes, stirring gently to chill and dilute the drink slightly.

Garnish: Express the oils of an orange twist over the drink, and then drop it into the glass, adding crushed walnuts.

Serve: Stir well, and enjoy!

Made in the USA
Las Vegas, NV
02 December 2024

13202926R00059